# California Missions

## Visiting All 21

## Paul Rallion

**California Missions**
Visiting All 21
Copyright © 2016 by Paul Rallion

*ISBN: 978-1-365-31336-3 (sc)*
*ISBN: 979-8-370-45914-6 (clr)*
*ISBN: 978-1-365-33272-2 (ebk)*

*1st Edition: August 16, 2016*
*2nd Edition: August 29, 2021*
*3rd Edition: November 20, 2023*

# Dedications

*To All Members of the Missions*
I dedicate this book to the founders of the missions, to the American Indians, to the people who made their restorations possible, and to the public who visits them.

I wish to thank my wife, Mary, and our daughter Anaïs, for visiting the 21 missions with me.

# Contents

# Introduction

I became more interested in the Old Spanish California Missions when my daughter Anaïs started attending school at one of the missions. As part of the curriculum in California, students do a mission project in the 4th grade: a brochure, a poster, a presentation, a model, a video, etc. The process made me curious about the rest of the missions. I decided it would be a great project (and vacation) to visit all of them.

We visited the missions in this order: the first 4 we did separate local trips. For the next 14 we did a weeklong trip from Los Angeles to San Francisco. The last 3 we did a weekend trip from Los Angeles to San Diego. In order to enjoy what they have to offer, I advise you to visit **no more than three** missions in one day. Some missions will take you a longer time to visit: San Luis Rey, San Juan Capistrano, and Santa Barbara. Others will require a shorter amount of time: San Buenaventura, Santa Inés, Soledad, Santa Cruz, Santa Clara, and San Rafael.

It is a good idea to plan for additional time to visit other attractions at the major cities along California: San Diego, Oceanside, Orange County, Los Angeles, Ventura, Santa Barbara, San Luis Obispo, Monterey, Santa Cruz, San Francisco, Napa, and Sonoma.

# Some History

*How did the term Indians come about?*
When Christopher Columbus discovered America, he thought he had arrived in "The Indies," the islands and land around the Indian Ocean, where he wanted to go originally. So, he named the inhabitants: "Indians."

Spain had experience with colonization. They knew that land could be claimed by establishing a mission. They sent padres, soldiers, and supplies to build them. The Spanish also knew that the Russians were exploring and maybe claiming North America's Pacific Coast. The missions' purpose was to strengthen the Spanish Empire in Upper California. Not having enough Spaniards in the New World, they chose the Franciscan religious order to:
1) Attract and Christianize the Native Californian (Indian) population, rather than conquer, but once converted, Indians were not allowed to leave the missions, and
2) Teach them new skills: farming, carpentry, making adobe bricks and tiles, soap, candles, wine, etc.

There were 8 **California Indian Groups** that lived in the areas where the missions were established:
1) Diegueño – San Diego Mission
2) Luiseño Tribe – San Luis Rey, San Juan Capistrano
3) Tongva (Gabrielino & Fernandeño) – San Gabriel & San Fernando Mission
4) Chumash – San Buenaventura, Santa Barbara, Santa Ines, La Purisima, San Luis Obispo Missions
5) Salinan – San Miguel, San Antonio de Padua

6) Esselen – Nuestra Señora de Soledad Mission

7) Ohlone, Yokuts – San Carlos Borromeo, San Juan Bautista, Santa Cruz, Santa Clara, San Jose, San Francisco Missions

8) Coast Miwok – San Rafael, Solano Missions.


**The Mission Era** lasted from 1769 to 1834, a period of 65 years. After Mexico gained independence from Spain in 1821, the missions were secularized in 1834, and their decline began. They were turned over to civil authorities and mission towns were turned into pueblos. The lands were supposed to be distributed to the California Natives. Instead, many of them were taken by politicians, their families and their friends. Most began to deteriorate, fell in despair, and were abandoned.

In 1859, President James Buchanan returned San Gabriel, San Juan Bautista, and Santa Cruz Missions to the Catholic Church. In 1865, President Abraham Lincoln signed a document that returned the rest of the missions to the Church. Sadly, President Lincoln was assassinated a few weeks later, and never visited California.

The Mission Era also affected native Californians in negative ways: the Spanish forced the Natives to change their ways of life. In addition, the Spanish brought diseases that killed thousands of native Californians. There was a sharp decline in native Californian population, from roughly 300,000 to only 20,000 after the Mission Era was over.


### The Gold Rush (1848–1855)

When James Marshall found gold at Sutter's Mill in Coloma, 90 miles from Sonoma, the news of gold brought approximately 300,000 people to California from the rest of the United States and abroad. The Gold Rush had severe effects on Native Californians and the Native American population's decline. California Indian groups were attacked and pushed off their lands by the gold-seekers, who called themselves "forty-niners," referring to the year 1849, the peak year of the Gold Rush.

**Notes:**
- Please verify the telephone number, physical address, web address, and museum hours of each mission before visiting, especially during Holidays.
- If you are a parent and your kid(s) are not in the 4th grade, I highly recommend this trip as an enjoyable and memorable vacation.

# General Facts

The California Missions in this book are listed in geographical order, starting from San Diego (South) to San Francisco Solano in Sonoma (North). I begin each mission with its address, phone number, website, hours of operation, and fun facts: the order in which it was founded, by whom, when, and who it was named after. I continue with my suggested time that it takes to visit each mission, things to look for, what's next with local recommendations, and the approximate time it takes you to get to the next mission.

At most of the missions, you first go into the gift shop to purchase your admission to the museum. Look at your tour map and plan your visit accordingly. I suggest holding off purchasing any souvenirs until the end of your tour of the mission. You usually end the tour back in the gift shop.

Even though some missions might look similar in some regards, no two missions are identical. However, most missions have the following:
-   Arched corridors
-   A Parish church or chapel
-   A museum with artifacts in rooms that were previously used for padres' headquarters, bedrooms, dining rooms, etc.
-   A bell tower
-   A patio with a garden and/or fountain
-   A cemetery

Many missions offer mass celebrations, many celebrate certain festivities, some missions have a school, and two of the missions are part of a State Historic Park.

# Other Interesting Facts:

All missions had 2 padres with 5 to 6 assigned soldiers. One padre would be in charge of the administration of the mission, and the other would be in charge of Religious education. Sometimes they would alternate roles.

Bells were rung at mealtimes, the call to work, the summons to worship, the announcement of baptisms and funerals, the approach of visitors or a ship, etc.

In some mission museums, you'll see replicas of interior rooms and furniture. Some may seem smaller than today's. Some doorframes seem lower as well. This is in part because people, in general, were shorter than we are today.

There was going to be a 22nd mission in Santa Rosa around 1827, but it never became a reality.

The construction of the missions was limited in the available materials. However, the buildings and facilities were impressive. In general, padres sought to emulate Spanish structures when building the missions.

Missions were damaged by earthquakes in 1804, 1812, 1925, fire, vandalism, the elements, abandonment, etc. The restoration of the missions has been a continuous effort, starting from paintings and photographs, to various groups investing in bringing the past back to their location.

The importance of horses in the establishment of the missions was great. In 1493, Christopher Columbus brought Spanish horses to the Americas, specifically to the Virgin Islands. In 1519, Hernan Cortés brought them to the mainland. The missions are about 30 miles apart, or during the mission era, the distance covered by horseback in one day.

# El Camino Real

Today's US Highway 101 roughly follows the unpaved path that linked all 21 missions between San Diego and Sonoma. I made this map to help you with the approximate time it takes to drive from one mission to the next (without traffic), according to Google Maps:

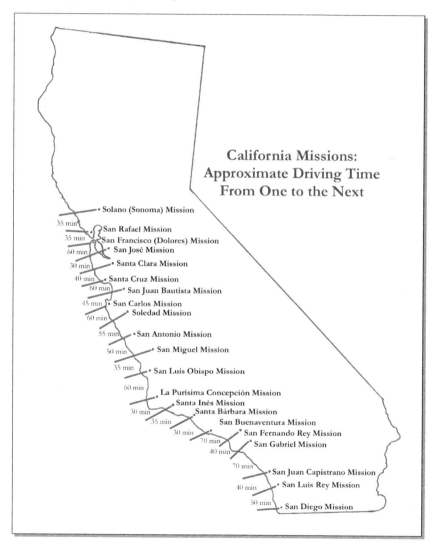

California Missions:
Approximate Driving Time
From One to the Next

• Solano (Sonoma) Mission
35 min
San Rafael Mission
35 min — San Francisco (Dolores) Mission
60 min • San José Mission
30 min • Santa Clara Mission
40 min • Santa Cruz Mission
60 min — • San Juan Bautista Mission
45 min • San Carlos Mission
60 min • Soledad Mission
55 min • San Antonio Mission
50 min • San Miguel Mission
35 min • San Luis Obispo Mission
60 min • La Purísima Concepción Mission
• Santa Inés Mission
30 min Santa Bárbara Mission
35 min San Buenaventura Mission
30 min • San Fernando Rey Mission
70 min • San Gabriel Mission
40 min
70 min • San Juan Capistrano Mission
40 min • San Luis Rey Mission
50 min • San Diego Mission

*Paul Rallion*

# 1. San Diego de Alcalá Mission

10818 San Diego Mission Road | San Diego, CA 92108
Phone: (619) 283-7319 | www.missionsandiego.org
Museum Hours: 9:00am - 4:00pm

*Fun Facts:*

San Diego de Alcalá, the 1st Mission, was founded by
Father Junípero Serra on July 16, 1769. The mission was
named after the Spanish Catholic saint Didacus of Alcalá.

San Diego Mission marked the start of the mission trail in
1769. Indians who rebelled against the new rules burned down
the mission. The mission was rebuilt in a quadrangle shape like
an army fort with thicker walls and tile roof. The first State
cemetery is located at this mission. The port of San Diego was
discovered by Juan Rodríguez Cabrillo in 1542.

When we arrived at this mission I thought, *Wow, this is where it all started!* However, the start was not easy: native Californians rebelled against Father Junipero Serra and they killed Father Luis Jayme, and two other Spaniards, and burned the mission. Father Serra organized the rebuilding and, 2 years later, a fire-proof adobe structure was built. The water supply was not sufficient, so the mission was relocated to its present site 6 miles inland, along the San Diego River.

*Visiting Time: (about 1-2 hours)*
Go into the gift shop to purchase your admission to the museum. As you start your tour to your left, you'll be able to enter a room that is believed to be for the two Padres living on the mission. Next, you'll enter the chapel, which emulates characteristics of Spanish churches and chapels. However, they were limited by the materials and the somewhat-trained labor.

As you exit the chapel you'll walk into an open garden with the Campanario (a wall with 5 bells) to your left, a popular picture location:

Whenever you see the bells at the missions, notice the bell sizes and their associated ringtones. There were distinct combinations to send different sound messages.

Finally, you'll make your way around to the museum, where you'll be able to appreciate precious artifacts, including pictures of the mission from the past. There is one particularly shocking picture, which shows the mission in ruins. The missions were not only rebuilt, but also beautifully restored. You'll also see 21 frames with the façades of all the California

Missions, all in white. As you exit the museum you can see the fountain in the middle of an open area as well as an example of a Native American hut. You can also visit an archaeological site.

### What's Next?

Consider spending time in San Diego. Visit the Cabrillo National Monument with great views, take a tour of San Diego Bay, visit local museums, and Downtown San Diego. For a historic feeling of San Diego, I recommend visiting Old Town San Diego for dining and souvenirs. Visit local theme parks (SeaWorld, San Diego Zoo Safari Park, and Legoland), but those would likely require an extra day per park, so plan accordingly.

San Diego Mission is located in the Mission Valley, 6 miles northeast of San Diego. It will take you about 50 minutes to get to the next mission: San Luis Rey de Francia.

# 2. San Luis Rey de Francia Mission

4050 Mission Avenue | San Luis Rey, CA 92068
Phone: (760) 757-3651 | www.sanluisrey.org
Museum Hours: 10:00am - 4:00pm

*Fun Facts:*

San Luis Rey de Francia, the 18th Mission, was founded by Father Fermín Lasuén on September 8, 1797. The mission was named after St. Louis IX, King of France, who was canonized (the only French King to become a Saint) in 1920 for his crusades to Egypt and the Holy Land.

The King of Missions, as it is known, was the last one founded by Father Fermín Lasuén. It was the largest and most populous mission: 2,700 Native Americans, 50,000 cattle and sheep, and 2,000 horses.

*Visiting Time: (about 1-2 hours)*

It's fun to be on your way to a mission and look around for it when you're almost there. It's nice to finally arrive and say: "There it is!" It's easy to see why it's called the King of the Missions: It's huge!

After you pay for your admission fee, you enter the museum with display rooms with various artifacts. You can proceed to a video room where you can enjoy an informational video of the mission. You then go to the Historic Church, the only mission with a dome over the crossing:

Next to the church is the cemetery. On the other side of the mission is where you can find the first pepper tree planted in California. There is no access to the retreat garden, but you can view the tree on the right-hand side in the picture below:

Have you seen this picture before?

After viewing the hundreds of pictures that I took during our trip to the missions, it only made sense to select this one as the book's cover.

Across from the mission is the "Lavanderia," or Laundry, where mission members bathed and washed their clothes. When you go downstairs, you will be able to see the dry aqueducts that once saw plenty of water flow through.

One key ingredient in the success of this mission was the friendly Luiseño Tribe. They made adobe bricks and tiles under the direction of Father Peyri, who spent over 30 years at the mission. Before the mission era ended, Father Peyri returned to Spain without saying goodbye to the Luiseños. When the Luiseños found out of his departure, they followed Father Peyri to San Diego, who was on a ship departing from the San Diego port.

*What's Next?*

If you have time, consider visiting Oceanside to grab a bite to eat, shopping, visiting the pier, or just walking around town.

San Luis Rey Mission is located 5 miles east of Oceanside. It will take you about 40 minutes to get to the next mission: San Juan Capistrano.

# 3. San Juan Capistrano Mission

26801 Ortega Highway | San Juan Capistrano, CA 92675
Phone: (949) 234-1300 | www.missionsjc.com
Museum Hours: 9:00am - 5:00pm
Mondays: Closed

*Fun Facts:*

San Juan Capistrano, the 7th Mission, was founded by
Father Junípero Serra on November 1, 1776. The mission was
named after St. John of Capistrano, Naples, an Italian
theologian who was born in 1386, after the bubonic plague
(1346 to 1353), the most fatal pandemic in human history.

The mission is home to the Serra chapel of 1777, the only
surviving church (and the oldest church in California) where
Father Serra said mass. The first vineyard in California was at
this mission, which produced the first wine in the State.

*Visiting Time: (about 2 hours)*

This Mission Basilica pictured in this section is off-site, located on Acjachema St, a 5-minute walk to the mission entrance located on Ortega Highway.

This mission is called the "Jewel of the Missions," and it is exquisitely maintained. You get an optional audio hand-held device with your entry fee. You also receive a map of the mission to play any available audio description. The map also contains specific items designed for 4th graders. You can spend some time admiring the beautifully landscaped gardens (front and central courtyards). I suggest you go through the museum rooms and the Mission Industrial Center in a clockwise direction. You will then arrive at the Serra Chapel, the last church where Father Serra celebrated mass:

As you exit the chapel, you end up in the Sacred Garden, where you can admire the mission's bell wall. We were told these bells came from the bell tower of the Great Stone Church. The Stone Church collapsed in a massive earthquake in 1812. Unfortunately, this happened during mass, killing 40 people. The four original bells were hung in a bell wall the following year:

According to legend, "El regreso de las golondrinas," (The Return of the Swallows), the swallows return on St. Joseph's Day in March, after their long journey to Argentina, around October.

As you continue your tour away from the courtyard, towards the east gate, you can walk around the ruins of the Great Stone Church. You can walk up close to appreciate what was the altar of the church and its remains as you listen to the audio segment corresponding to the collapse of the church.

You're not far from the exit, which is the gift shop, where you can purchase a souvenir.

*What's Next?*

Consider spending some time in San Juan Capistrano; there are some nice restaurants around the area.

San Juan Capistrano Mission is located in the Village of San Juan Capistrano, 65 miles north of San Diego. It will take you about 1 hour and 10 minutes to get to the next mission: San Gabriel.

Optional: Halfway between San Juan Capistrano and San Gabriel Mission, sits Disneyland and California Adventure theme parks in Orange County. A visit to those parks, as well as other attractions, would require additional days.

# 4. San Gabriel Arcángel Mission

427 S. Junipero Serra Drive | San Gabriel, CA 91776
Phone: (626) 457-3035 | www.sangabrielmissionchurch.org
Museum Hours: 8:00am to 4:00pm
Mondays: Closed

*Fun Facts:*

San Gabriel Arcángel, the 4th Mission, was founded by Father Cambón and Father Somera on September 8, 1771. The mission was named after the Archangel Gabriel, God's messenger.

San Gabriel Mission was known as the "Pride of the Missions." It had one quarter of the wealth of all missions in stock and grain. One of the six bells in the Campanario weighs about one ton.

*Visiting Time: (about 1-2 hours)*

You'll find the entrance to the Museum directly accessible from the parking lot. After you purchase your admission, work your way around clockwise. You'll go through a cemetery where the first Indian of the mission, Antonio, is buried, along with numerous Padres. Enter the chapel from a side door, where you'll appreciate six statues brought from Spain in 1791.

Don't leave the chapel without taking a look at the copper baptismal font where the 25,000+ baptisms were performed between the years 1771 and 1834.

I recommend visiting the "Court of the Missions," a display of all 21 missions made in 1930. It is found to the right of the open fireplaces, as you come from the display corridor:

Walk around the outside of the chapel, where you'll see the Campanario, a unique sidewall with long, narrow windows. The fountain is located outside (like Buenaventura Mission). A few feet away from it, you can see a display of Chapman's Millrace, which carried water from nearby rivers to the mission, and made its success and wealth possible.

San Gabriel Mission was known for its wine. You can see a pergola, along its courtyard, where these grapes still grow. At its peak, the vineyards at San Gabriel covered about 170 acres, producing around 50,000 gallons of wine per year.

At a given point, San Gabriel Mission was the top producer and supplier of soap and candles to most of the other missions. There are 4 boilers with a total capacity exceeding 2,500 gallons. This is what they look like today:

San Gabriel Mission celebrates its yearly "La Fiesta de San Gabriel" over Labor day weekend.

*What's Next?*

Consider taking an extra day or two to visit Los Angeles. There are many places you can visit, like Downtown Los Angeles, the Griffith Observatory, Hollywood and its surroundings, countless museums such as the Getty Center and Villa, etc., so plan accordingly. For a historic feeling of Los Angeles, visit Olvera Street.

San Gabriel Mission is located in the city of San Gabriel, 10 miles from Los Angeles. It will take you about 40 minutes to the next mission: San Fernando Rey.

# 5. San Fernando Rey Mission

15151 San Fernando Mission Blvd | Mission Hills, CA 91345
Phone: (818) 361-0186
www.missionscalifornia.com/keyfacts/san-fernando-rey.html
Museum Hours: 9:00am - 4:30pm

*Fun Facts:*

San Fernando Rey, the 17th Mission, was founded by Father Fermín Lasuén on September 8, 1797. The mission was named after Ferdinand III of Castile, the King of Spain in the 1200s.

The Convento is the largest freestanding adobe building in California. It is a two-story building, 243 feet (74 m) long by 50 feet (15 m) wide The Hearst Foundation gave a large monetary gift to restore the mission in the 1940s.

*Visiting Time: (about 1-2 hours)*

After paying your fee to visit the mission, you see the water fountain, a focal point in the middle of the east garden.

Make your way to the Convento, where the padres quarters and a guest house are located. In the Convento you will find a rich collection of displays, paintings, artifacts, books, and how roof tiles were made. There is a series of small paintings of all 21 missions in color.

The San Fernando Mission did well in cattle ranching and farming. It produced corn, wheat, olive oil, wine, and brandy.

Try finding the access to go downstairs to view the wine cellar. It is a dark and cold room, perfect for storing and aging wine. A unique display among the missions: wine barrels and a wine press:

After pressing the grapes, the juice collected was stored in these barrels located in this cold room for fermentation. Wine-making in the missions was necessary for the celebration of mass, rather than importing it. The wine represents the "Blood of Christ" during mass. It was the table beverage of the padres. Brandy, a spirit distilled from wine, was also consumed. The three largest mission producers of wine were: Mission San Juan Capistrano (Viñedo Madre, or Mother Vineyard), Mission San Gabriel, and Mission San Diego.

As you exit the Convento, work your way clockwise to the west garden. Continue walking towards the end where you'll arrive at The Old Mission Church, a popular picture spot. This is what the beautiful golden altar looks like:

As you exit the mission church, you can walk to the Bob Hope Memorial, the resting place for the Hope family. Bob Hope was a comedian who entertained American troops, both at home and abroad.

Make your way back towards the gift shop, passing through workshops: blacksmith, pottery, etc.

San Fernando Mission celebrates its "Fiestas" with arts, crafts, and food in June.

*What's Next?*

San Fernando Rey Mission is located about 50 miles west of Los Angeles, in the city of San Fernando. It will take you about 1 hour and 10 minutes to get to the next mission: San Buenaventura.

# 6. San Buenaventura Mission

211 East Main Street | Ventura, CA 93001
Phone: (805) 648-4496 | www.sanbuenaventuramission.org
Museum Hours: 10:00am - 5:00pm

*Fun Facts:*

San Buenaventura, the 9th Mission, was founded by Father
Junípero Serra on March 31, 1782. The mission was named
after Saint Bonaventure, an Italian priest from the 1200s.

This was Father Serra's last mission. There are two
wooden bells, the only ones of their type in California. The
Chumash Indians were expert boat builders, a good match
when you live at this mission close to the ocean.

*Visiting Time: (about 1 hour)*

A beautiful mission surrounded by a busy city. It is hard to imagine what the surroundings must have looked like when you have a busy street in front of it. The gift shop entrance on Main St.

What I'm looking for as I enter the museum are the wooden bells. We were told they may have been temporary bells as perhaps the real bells never arrived. Here they are:

As we exited the museum we moved on to the garden where you can see a small altar and an olive press.

The first olive tree was planted in San Diego Mission, and consequently in all other missions. Olives were collected, placed in the olive press, powered by a burro. Olive oil was produced storing the juice in jars to be used for cooking.

We took a moment to pose next to Father Serra's statue:

As a side note, before (or after) visiting this mission, consider visiting the Serra Cross (known as the Cross on the Hill or the Grant Park Cross), about 1 mile away. It is a Christian cross on "La Loma de la Cruz," in the Serra Cross Park. From there you can appreciate the view of downtown Ventura, the Santa Barbara Channel, and the Anacapa and Santa Cruz Islands. The first cross was erected in 1782, at the time of the founding of Mission San Buenaventura.

The Chumash Indians are said to have frequented the Channel Islands, which is now the Channel Islands National Park. It can be visited by ferry to enjoy camping, kayaking or hiking. –Note: there are no hotels on the islands.

Next, visit the mission chapel:

After viewing the chapel, you can get back to the center garden and then to the museum and gift shop.

*What's Next?*

If you have the time, consider taking a walk down Main Street, where you'll find plenty of restaurants and shops.

San Buenaventura Mission is located in the city of Ventura, 60 miles north of Los Angeles. It will take you about 30 minutes to get to the next mission: Santa Bárbara.

# 7. Santa Bárbara Mission

2201 Laguna Street | Santa Barbara, CA 93105
Phone: (805) 682-4713 | www.santabarbaramission.org
Museum Hours: 9:30am - 4:00pm

*Fun Facts:*

Santa Bárbara, the 10th Mission, was founded by Father
Fermín Lasuén on December 16, 1786. The mission was
named after St. Barbara, the patron of artillerymen and miners.

Santa Bárbara Mission is known as the "Queen of the
Missions." It is the first Cathedral in California, which still
serves as a parish church today. It is the only mission with 2
similar towers. The fountain and lavadero (laundry area) are
original. The church has the largest paintings of any mission.

*Visiting Time: (about 1-2 hours)*

This mission is one of my favorites. There is ample parking and a large open area where you can appreciate the impressive mission façade, a fountain and the Lavanderia, or "Laundry" where mission members bathed and washed their clothes:

The water came down from a creek about two miles away. The aqueduct that the padres designed for this mission was one of the most advanced of all the missions.

Once you pay your admission fee, you walk alongside the central garden. The garden itself was not accessible, but it can be viewed as you walk around the quadrangle, along the surrounding rooms that were used as workshops. There is a video room where you can watch a film featuring the mission.

The chapel, or the first California Cathedral, contains the largest paintings of any mission, painted by Mexican artists from the 18th and 19th century:

Following the mission map provided, you are directed back to the museum after exiting the chapel.

The sheer size of the mission façade was a way to establish a strong presence in Alta California for possible Russian settlers.

One item that caught my attention was a telescope. The sign explained that this brass telescope was given to the superior of the mission, Father Jose Maria Romo. The telescope was made in Paris, purchased in Egypt, and was likely used to scan the harbor for arriving ships.

After you view these precious artifacts you are directed to the gift shop, busy with shoppers at the time we did our own shopping.

*What's Next?*

Consider spending the night (or at least some time) in Santa Bárbara and take a walk in Downtown Santa Bárbara. Rent a bike to enjoy the coastal bike path.

Santa Bárbara Mission is located 35 minutes west of San Buenaventura. It will take you about 35 minutes to get to the next mission: Santa Inés.

# 8. Santa Inés Mission

1760 Mission Drive | Solvang, CA 93463
Phone: (805) 688-4815 | www.missionsantaines.org
Museum Hours: 9:00am - 4:30pm

*Fun Facts:*

Santa Inés, the 19th Mission, was founded by Father Tápis on September 15, 1804. The mission was named after St. Agnes of Rome, a martyr of the early Christian church.

Santa Inés was not completely abandoned after secularization in 1834. California's first seminary (Our Lady of Refuge), was built in 1844. The Hearst foundation donated funds for its restoration. We were told that the city of Solvang was built around the mission.

*Visiting Time: (about 1-2 hours)*

We had been to the city of Solvang, but did not visit the mission at that time. We're glad to be back. There is a large parking lot from which you can easily access the gift shop. As with most other missions, it's nice to look at the arched corridor:

When you pay for your admission and enter the first room, you can find a history sheet in five languages: English, Spanish, Italian, German, and French. As someone who likes languages, I wish other missions did the same!

Next is a location within the museum where you can see a model of the mission. This is something most other missions have in display. Another room that is common among most missions is a place displaying vestments: robes worn by the priests during ceremonies.

Proceed to the chapel, where the Stations of the Cross are depicted on the walls:

Inside the quadrangle, you can walk around and relax in the beautiful garden with the gorgeous fountain in the center.

When you exit the chapel towards the central garden, make a right and go around the chapel to visit the mission cemetery. You can see the three-bell tower at the back. The graveyard you can see on the next picture is the final resting place of more than 1,500 Indians:

Mission of the Passes: The location of Santa Inés was difficult to access. After visitors battled the San Marcos Pass, the Refugio Pass or the Gaviota Pass (El Camino Real), they were welcomed warmly.

Mission Santa Inés suffered damages from the great earthquake of 1812 and the Chumash revolt of 1824 when the Indians aggressively protested treatment by the military guards.

*What's Next?*

Consider spending some time in the Danish town of Solvang: walk around or take a trolley tour. The city is relatively small and can be enjoyed in a day or so.

Santa Inés Mission is located in the city of Solvang, 35 minutes west of Santa Barbara. It will take you about 30 minutes to get to the next mission: La Purísima Concepción.

# 9. La Purísima Concepción Mission

2295 Purisima Road | Lompoc, CA 93436
Phone: (805) 733-3713 | www.lapurisimamission.org
Tour Hours: 9:00am - 5:00pm
Entry fee by vehicle: cars or buses

*Fun Facts:*

La Purísima Concepción de María Santísima, the 11th Mission, was founded by Father Fermín Lasuén on December 8, 1787. The mission was named after the Immaculate Conception of Most Holy Mary.

La Purísima was the only mission built on a linear series of buildings with 37 rooms. Some of the specialties at the mission were candle-making and weaving. On December 8th, there is a candle ceremony in celebration of the date the mission was established. There is a large animal area: horses, cattle, burros, sheep, etc. This mission is now a State Historic Park.

*Visiting Time: (about 2-3 hours)*

This mission is unique and one of the highlights of the visit to the 21 mission. The sign on the highway invites you to drive into the parking lot. When we arrived, there was no parking attendant. Instead, there were envelopes for visitors to fill out and deposit the parking fee in a box. There is a new visitor center and exhibit hall. Walk around the parking lot towards two adobe white houses. Then, make a left turn, where you will see the mission:

I took this panoramic picture to show the sheer size of the mission. From behind that point you see a sign that reads: "El Camino Real, the Royal Road. El Camino Real linked the mission, presidios, and pueblos, and it varied with the travel conditions."

We asked one of the park rangers how to visit this mission. He advised us to walk along the fenced animal area first and then work our way back through the buildings.

The great earthquake of December, 1812, destroyed the mission buildings, along with severe flooding. In 1813, the mission was rebuilt in the Valley of Watercress, about 3 miles from its original site.

The mission's water systems are still visible. Up towards the back we saw a Lavanderia, or "Laundry" where mission members bathed and washed their clothes.

One thing that amazed me at this mission was what appear to be latrines. Perhaps the same kinds of latrines were used in other missions, although what I have seen displayed at other missions is chamber pots. In any case, here is a picture:

Next was the chapel, which had no pews at the time of our visit, only a few benches around the perimeter.

At the end of the tour, behind the Campanario, you see the Cemetery Camposanto, in memory of early Californians who are buried there. From there, find your way out next to the animal area, and back to the parking lot.

Tip: Arrive at the mission much earlier than 4 pm; otherwise, you won't be able to see everything in the mission.

*What's Next?*

La Purísima Concepción Mission is located 5 miles north of Lompoc. It will take you about 1 hour to get to the next mission: San Luis Obispo.

Optional: You can make a stop at Pismo Beach. Enjoy a quick stop to shop, or relax at the beach.

# 10. San Luis Obispo de Tolosa Mission

751 Palm Street | San Luis Obispo, CA 93401
Phone: (805) 781-8220 | www.missionsanluisobispo.org
Museum Hours: 11:00am - 4:30pm
Mondays and Tuesdays: Closed

*Fun Facts:*

San Luis Obispo de Tolosa, the 5th Mission, was founded by Father Junípero Serra on September 1, 1772. The mission was named after St. Louis, Bishop of Toulouse, France, a 14th century Franciscan.

The mission is located in the well-watered Valley of the Bears. San Luis Obispo Mission was one of the only lucky missions that did not have to relocate.

*Visiting Time: (about 1-2 hours)*

When you arrive at the Mission Plaza you see a small bear fountain. This area was known for an abundance of bears, which were hunted to alleviate shortages of food in 1772.

Make your way to the chapel upstairs. As you approach the altar you'll notice its uniqueness among the mission in its design. The church was designed in an "L" shape, with two separate aisles at a 90-degree angle when viewed from the altar. In other words, if you face the altar you can see the side section to your right, which looks directly at it, rather than being a side aisle.

As with many mission chapels, the Stations of the Cross are depicted on the walls:

From the chapel, go to the museum and gift shop. As you go through the museum, you can see paintings of Chumash life. You will also see several displays of vestments, antique room setups, furniture arrangements, paintings, etc.

San Luis Obispo Mission was the first mission to use red roof tiles to protect against attacks by Indians who used flaming arrows. These flaming arrows set the tule roof on fire; the padres decided to start making roof tiles locally. This type of tile became a symbol of California missions.

As you walk through the garden, you can appreciate (and get shade from) grape arbors. Father Luis Antonio Martínez, who served the mission for 30+ years, grew a large vineyard that supplied wine to other missions.

There are three bells in the bell tower (replicas), and three bells hung outside (original):

Father Luis Antonio Martínez ordered bells from Lima, Peru.

The city of San Luis Obispo grew from the location of the mission, as was the case with San Diego, San Gabriel (Los Angeles), San Fernando, Ventura, Santa Bárbara, Carmel, and San Francisco.

*What's Next?*

Consider spending some time in the Downtown Historic District in San Luis Obispo, which is a walking distance from the mission, across the San Luis Obispo Creek. You can spend some time visiting shops and restaurants.

San Luis Obispo Mission is located in San Luis Obispo, 1 hour north of Lompoc. It will take you about 35 minutes to get to the next mission: San Miguel de Arcángel.

# 11. San Miguel Arcángel Mission

775 Mission Street | San Miguel, CA 93451
Phone: (805) 467-3256 | www.missionsanmiguel.org
Museum Hours: 10:00am - 4:00pm
Tuesdays and Wednesdays: Closed

*Fun Facts:*

San Miguel Arcángel, the 16th Mission, was founded by
Father Fermín Lasuén on July 25, 1797. The mission was
named after St. Michael the Archangel, who is associated with
courage, protection, and divine intervention.

This mission has no bell tower; its 1-ton bell rang out from
a wooden platform. It is one of the best-preserved interiors.
There is an eye at the altar and painted shells on the sidewall in
the chapel. The roof tiles show finger markings.

*Visiting Time: (about 1 hour)*

As you walk in, you can see the hanging 1-ton bell. Farther ahead, there was a carreta (cart) with roof tiles. I was looking for the finger markings on the roof tiles, as I had seen on one of the videos from Huell Howser:

The fountain is a nice welcoming point ahead, visually decorated by the arched corridor on the right. We went to the gift shop to pay for our admission fee to the museum.

As we went through the different mission rooms with multiple displays (including a large model of the mission), we noticed how well preserved these interiors are. These displays show daily life at the mission, the padres' living quarters, displays of chairs, tables, beds, built-in cabinets, as well as other paintings and artifacts.

In 1806, a devastating fire destroyed the church and several buildings, where many products were lost, such as grains and other farming products, wool, and hides. Ten years later, the new church was built with adobe blocks. The walls were built six feet thick.

The chapel has some peculiar characteristics, unique to this mission. At the center top of the altar you can see "the eye of God," symbolizing the God that the Indians could now believe in to be watching them, as well as protecting them. On both sides of the picture you can see paintings on the wall of abalone shells representing baptism: purification and admission to the Christian Church.

What you see are original paintings, which have survived the test of time:

From the chapel, you can visit the cemetery, the final resting place of about 2,000 Indians. Looking at the map that I received at the gift shop, the cemetery runs parallel to the chapel and both (the chapel and the cemetery) appear to be about the same size. From the cemetery, you can walk out of the mission; one of the few where you don't end up back in the gift shop.

San Miguel Mission celebrates its birthday with an annual Fiesta the 3rd Sunday in September.

*What's Next?*

San Miguel Mission is located 35 miles north of San Luis Obispo, 10 miles north of Paso Robles. It will take you about 50 minutes to get to the next mission: San Antonio de Padua.

# 12. San Antonio de Padua Mission

Ft. Hunter-Liggett Reservation | Jolon, CA 93928
Phone: (831) 385-4478 | www.missionsanantonio.net
Museum Hours: 10:00am - 4:00pm
Mondays and Tuesdays: Closed

*Fun Facts:*

San Antonio de Padua, the 3rd Mission, was founded by Father Junípero Serra on July 14, 1771. The mission was named after Saint Anthony, a Portuguese saint from the 1200s.

The mission is surrounded by the Fort Hunter Liggett Military Reservation, in which US troops have been training since World War II. San Antonio Mission is the site of the first marriage in California. The Hearst foundation gave $50,000 to start restorations in 1948.

*Visiting Time: (about 1-2 hours)*

Getting to this mission is quite an experience. You have to drive on winding roads and go through checkpoints in the military reservation. It is also one of the highlights of the 21 mission visit. Like in La Purísima Mission, being in a remote location, it makes you feel like you're standing in the past. At the time of our visit, the mission was undergoing restoration. Half of the quadrangle was being re-roofed, and the left bell was missing.

After parking in the dirt lot, we walked to the brick façade. On the porch, you can read the sign: "First marriage in California in 1773." So, my wife and I posed for a picture:

Next, we went to the chapel. The colors are a soft yellow, orange and blue:

The quadrangle houses the Padres' quarters, a wine room with wine barrels like San Fernando Rey, and other workshop rooms: textile, olive press, a mission model, and paintings.

The story goes that before its founding, Father Serra was over enthusiastic: After unloading the mules and hanging a bell from a tree, Father Serra started calling on people to come to the Holy Church. A large cross was later erected, and Father Serra celebrated mass. He gave a small gift to a local young Indian, and that attracted the attention of local Indians. The Salinans were friendly, which helped in building a good relationship, which in turn helped the mission flourish.

Missions thrived when a good water source could be found. The first location did not supply enough water, so the mission had to be moved a few miles. The San Antonio river proved to be a better water source for the mission needs, such as washing, cooking, drinking, and irrigation. You can appreciate the fountain in the center of the quadrangle:

The fort is the largest US Army Reserve post, and it is used as a training facility for field and fire exercises. It was named after General Hunter Liggett, who served in the US Military for 42 years in the American Indian Wars, Spanish–American War, Philippine–American War, and World War I. He received the following awards: Army Distinguished Service Medal, Legion of Honor (France), and Croix de guerre (France).

*What's Next?*

San Antonio Mission is located 50 miles north of the San Miguel Mission, 6 miles from Jolon. It will take you about 55 minutes to get to the next mission: Nuestra Señora de la Soledad.

# 13. Nuestra Señora de la Soledad Mission

36641 Fort Romie Road | Soledad, CA 93960
Phone: (831) 678-2586 | www.missionsoledad.com
Museum Hours: 10:00am - 4:00pm
Mondays and Holidays: Closed

*Fun Facts:*

Nuestra Señora de Soledad, the 13th Mission, was founded by Father Fermín Lasuén on October 9, 1791. The mission was named after Our Lady of Solitude, a name given to the Virgin Mary contemplating the death of her son, Jesus.

The name Soledad (Solitude) was not given for the feeling and appearance of the location and surroundings, even though it would have been accurate. The mission was abandoned for almost a century.

*Visiting Time: (about 1-2 hours)*

After driving in desolate areas for almost 1 hour in 105 F in the summer, it was nice to arrive at the sign: "Soledad Mission." The weather here was windy and in the 80's Fahrenheit. We parked in the dirt parking lot and walked to the mission. There is no bell tower, but a bell hung on the side of the chapel. We went to the gift shop, purchased our admission and went through the museum rooms: Native American paintings, the original mission bell (cast in Mexico in 1799), artifacts, pottery, and antique plates.

We then went to the cozy, narrow chapel:

Exiting the last room of the building and walking around the corner was a shocking experience. There is no quadrangle as in most missions. There is a sign that reads: "Site of Original Church – Dedicated October 9, 1791 and Destroyed by Floods in 1828."

Mission buildings suffered damages from the great earthquake of 1812. The church area still has the original tile floor.

This mission had difficulty growing, but it prospered slowly thanks to the Salinas river, which provided water for daily living and irrigation for the crops. However, the same river also overflowed, causing damage to the mission buildings.

The area is windy, cold, and damp. A respiratory epidemic killed a few dozen people at the mission in 1802.

For the same reason, the mission had a high turnover of padres: in forty years there were around thirty different priests serving at Soledad Mission.

Even though most mission quadrangles are restorations, I didn't expect to see ruins like these with signs of what they were: Indian Workshops, Carpenter Shops, etc.

*What's Next?*

Nuestra Señora de la Soledad Mission is located 50 minutes north of the San Antonio Padua Mission, 2 miles from the town of Soledad. It will take you about 1 hour to get to the next mission: San Carlos Borromeo de Carmelo.

# 14. San Carlos Borromeo Mission

3080 Rio Road | Carmel, CA 93923
Phone: (831) 624-1271 | www.carmelmission.org
Museum Hours: 9:30am - 4:30pm
Mondays and Tuesday: Closed

*Fun Facts:*

San Carlos Borromeo, the 2nd Mission, was founded by
Father Junípero Serra on June 3, 1770. The mission was
named after Saint Charles Borromeo, archbishop of Milan,
Italy, in the 16th century.

Mission San Carlos Borromeo served as the headquarters
for all the missions between 1770 and 1803. Father Serra and
Father Lasuén are buried there. It was the first mission built of
stone. The façade holds a star-shaped window. It is the only
mission church with an arched ceiling.

*Visiting Time: (about 1-2 hours)*

This is one of my favorite missions. As soon as you arrive you can see the great church and its star-shaped window from the parking lot gate —can you tell it's slightly crooked? We went over to the visitor's entrance and museum store to purchase our admission.

First, we wanted to visit the stunning church and Fr. Serra's and Fr. Lasuén's graves. When we walked up to the altar we were shocked to see original pieces of wood from Father Junípero Serra's casket. They are displayed on your right-hand side as you face the altar.

The next point of interest is a beautiful sculpture of Father Serra's casket surrounded by missionaries' statues:

As we continued our tour through the museum rooms we were able to appreciate other displays such as vestments, artifacts, etc. There is a series of stunning pictures of the mission from the past: rescued from ruins, the missions building standing alone surrounded by vegetation, and a picture of Carmel Mission through time. These pictures take you back to the past the way this mission was more than two centuries ago.

Parallel to the Mission Basilica you can visit the cemetery, and like other missions mentioned before, the cemetery land is about the same size as the church land.

In the quadrangle near the fountain, you can see a tall cross. We were told this is where pieces of Father Serra's

Cross were found in excavations of the mission ruins. As you can see from the picture, it was undergoing renovations at the time of our visit.

In 1960, Pope John XXIII named Mission Carmel a Minor Basilica.

*What's Next?*

Consider taking extra time to visit Carmel Beach, Downtown Carmel, do the 17-mile drive, and a day trip to the Monterey Bay Aquarium (2-3 hours), Cannery Row, and Fisherman's Wharf, so plan accordingly.

San Carlos Borromeo Mission is located in the village of Carmel, 5 miles from Monterey. It will take you about 45 minutes to get to the next mission: San Juan Bautista.

# 15. San Juan Bautista Mission

406 Second St Old Mission San Juan Bautista
San Juan Bautista, CA 95045
Phone: (831) 623-2127 | www.oldmissionsjb.org
Museum Hours: 9:00am - 4:00pm
Mondays and Tuesday: Closed

*Fun Facts:*

San Juan Bautista, the 15th Mission, was founded by Father
Fermín Lasuén on June 24, 1797. The mission was named
after St. John the Baptist, the forerunner of Jesus.

This mission sits on the San Andreas Fault (Pacific &
North American Plates). Father Pedro Tápis taught Indians to
sing here, so the mission became known as "The Mission of
Music." The movie Vertigo was filmed there. An original
1850's town surrounds the mission.

*Visiting Time: (about 1-2 hours)*

Arriving at any mission can take you back in time. This mission is no different, except you get that feeling *before* you get to the mission. You can admire the historic 1850's buildings located in the only original Spanish plaza in the State. The Plaza San Juan Bautista houses the Plaza Hotel (1814), the Zenneta House, or the Plaza Hall (1868), and the Plaza Stable (1874).

Make your way to the mission museum, which is the first door on the left. From here you can see the beautiful arched corridor. As you walk through the museum you'll see several gorgeous displays of furniture and several artifacts, but most importantly, you'll see choir books written by Father Tápis before 1825.

Exit the museum to the nicely kept gardens, where you can take in fresh air while you take a break. From the garden, there is a side door to the largest and only mission church with three aisles:

San Juan Bautista Mission grew quickly. The land was favorable and the Indian population (Ohlone) friendly. The church was built to accommodate its growth and then expanded to have three isles and a capacity for over one thousand people.

Exit the church through the main door at the back. Make a quick left around the campanario and you'll find a small door to the cemetery. It is the far right arch you see when looking at the façade.

Make your way back to the cemetery door, walk past the

front of the church and on your left hand side, look for the "Original Route, El Camino Real" deck. Here you can see an unspoiled section of El Camino Real (the Royal Road). A few steps away, look for the "San Andreas Fault Exhibit & El Camino Real Earthquake Walk."

San Juan Bautista Mission celebrates a Virgen de Guadalupe fiesta every year in December.

*What's Next?*

San Juan Bautista Mission is located 45 minutes north of Monterey. It will take you about 1 hour to get to the next mission: Santa Cruz.

# 16. Santa Cruz Mission

126 High Street | Santa Cruz, CA 95060
Phone: (831) 426-5686
www.holycrosssantacruz.com/mission-santa-cruz
Museum Hours: 10:00am - 4:00pm
Tuesdays and Wednesdays: Closed

*Fun Facts:*

Santa Cruz, the 12th Mission, was founded by Father Fermín Lasuén on September 28, 1791. The mission was named, not after a saint, but after the Holy Cross.

Also known as "La Misión de la Exaltación de la Santa Cruz" (The Mission of the Exaltation of the Holy Cross), it was named the Hard Luck Mission. In 1931, Gladys Sullivan Doyle built a half-size replica with her own money, about 75 yards from the original site.

*Visiting Time: (about 1-2 hours)*

This is where my daughter Anaïs did her mission project in the 4th grade. She picked it because of its nickname: Hard Luck Mission. We found parking on the street, and visited the gift shop and museum where there are vestments, books from the mission, a Spanish crucifix, paintings, and chalices used for the service of the altar in the church during mass.

Next, we went to the mission church where you see a phrase in Latin: "We Adore You Christ and We Bless You Because Through Your Cross You Have Redeemed the World." I wish my dad could've been with us to read it to us. He spoke 9 languages: French, Spanish, English, German, Russian, Tagalog, Portuguese, Italian, and Latin.

You can then visit the small garden, where you can see the statue of Father Serra, and a small fountain:

The mission padres were forced to accept the Governor's orders to establish a nearby pueblo named Branciforte. The population was mostly a community of criminals who came from Mexico. That did not go well, as the thieves stole land from the Indians. Mission Santa Cruz had the lowest population of all the Missions, at about 500.

Another instance of Hard Luck was the announcement of an evil pirate's arrival who had vandalized Monterey. The governor ordered the padres to flee to Soledad Mission with valuables. While the padres were gone, the bandits from Branciforte helped themselves to what was left in the mission.

Quickly after secularization, the mission fell in despair. The earthquake of 1857 destroyed the church.

After visiting the mission replica built in 1931, go around the block to the left and visit the Mission Santa Cruz State

History Park. Here you will find an authentic adobe building, and various displays of American Indian housing and workshops. You can see displays of bedrooms, a kitchen, as well as artifacts for herding, weaving, tile making, etc.

As of the time of this writing, the park is open Thursday through Monday, from 10am to 4pm. Call the park to confirm: (831) 425-5849.

*What's Next?*

Consider spending some time in Downtown Santa Cruz, a short drive from the mission. Try to include in your itinerary the Santa Cruz Beach Boardwalk and the Mystery Spot!

Santa Cruz Mission is located in the city of Santa Cruz. It will take you about 40 minutes to get to the next mission: Santa Clara de Asís.

# 17. Santa Clara de Asís Mission

500 El Camino Real | Santa Clara, CA 95053
Phone: (408) 554-4023 | www.scu.edu/missionchurch
Mission Office Hours: 7:00am - 7:00pm

*Fun Facts:*

Santa Clara de Asís, the 8th Mission, was founded by Father Junípero Serra on January 12, 1777. The mission was named after Saint Claire of Assisi, a 13th century Italian nun, an early companion of St. Francis. Santa Clara was the first mission christened after a woman.

It is the only mission to become part of a university: Santa Clara University, the oldest university in California, founded in 1851. The bell tower contains the original bells sent from Spain, and are said to be rung at 8:30 pm as they have been for 225 years.

*Visiting Time: (about 1 hour)*

Getting to this mission is different, because you're actually going to a university campus. Also, finding parking may be difficult because students may be going to class. However, I learned that if you tell the parking attendant that you're visiting the mission you will have access to a special parking lot.

The mission serves two functions: 1) as the chapel of the campus, and 2) as a main attraction to visitors.

The façade of the mission chapel has reproduced the painting of the original church(es) into tri-dimensional decorations.

The cross you see in front of the mission chapel is the original one from 1777, used in all previous churches.

Before you arrive at the mission you see the fountain with the mission chapel in the background:

The mission chapel interior is stunning:

Around the chapel area you see informative signs about the mission. One explains that this is the third site of the mission, and this is the fifth chapel. The chapels had to be rebuilt due to fires, earthquakes, and floods.

There is another sign titled: "The Changing Church" that depicts four of the five churches: 1825 (no picture), 1835 (a painting), 1854 (a picture), 1883 (a shocking picture of it burning in 1926), and this mission church built in the 1970's.

After secularization, the Indian lands were given away. Later, they were returned to the church, which turned them over to the Jesuit order. The first University in California, Santa Clara University, was founded in 1851.

Next to the chapel is an original adobe building, with an adobe wall exposed:

Santa Clara University offers bachelor's degrees, master's degrees, and doctoral degrees through its 6 colleges: Arts and Sciences, Education and Counseling Psychology, Business, Engineering, Theology, and Law. It enrolls about 5,400 undergraduate students and about 3,300 postgraduate students. The University address is the same as the Mission's address.

*What's Next?*

Santa Clara Mission is located on the campus of the University of Santa Clara, city of Santa Clara. It will take you about 30 minutes to get to the next mission: San José.

# 18. San José Mission

43300 Mission Boulevard | Fremont, CA 94539
Phone: (510) 657-1797 | www.missionsanjose.org
Museum Hours: 10:00am - 4:30pm
Mondays and Tuesdays: Closed

*Fun Facts:*

San José, the 14th Mission, was founded by Father Fermín
Lasuén on June 11, 1797. The mission was named after Saint
Joseph, the husband of Mary, the mother of Jesus Christ.

It is located in Fremont, CA, but originally its lands
extended from San Jose to Oakland. During the Gold Rush,
the mission was used for lodging and as a general store. San
Jose Mission was the 2nd largest mission but almost completely
destroyed by an earthquake in 1868.

*Visiting Time: (about 1 hour)*

We almost didn't make it to this mission, due to traffic! Make sure you get there with plenty of time as mission Boulevard gets very busy around 4:00pm. We parked on the street a couple of blocks away and walked fast to the mission.

We came into the gift shop and the ladies told us we had about 30 minutes to visit the mission, but we felt it was sufficient. We took the exterior pictures last.

The museum has displays of Native Americans, hunting tools, grinding gear, baskets, vestments, a bed, music notation, and paintings. In the following picture, the redwood logs tied with coils of rawhide come from the Convento attic, part of the original mission construction:

From the museum, you can go to the patio where you'll find the fountain in the center and a statue of Father Serra:

The site of San José Mission was chosen for the abundance of natural resources in the area: plenty of water, fertile ground, and adobe soil that was used for building. Thousands of cattle roamed the mission lands, and wheat and other crops were planted and harvested. San Jose Mission was the 2nd largest mission, after San Luis Rey Mission.

As was the case with the choir books written by Father Tápis in San Juan Bautista Mission, Father Durán taught music to the Natives at San Jose Mission. He made the Indians successful in playing instruments and singing with a simplified method of music notation. As music enhances religious celebrations, it attracted many other Indians to the mission.

You can enter the 1869 church, a wonderful replica. The adobe church of 1809 was destroyed by an earthquake in 1868, and this wooden church replaced it:

Exit the church through the other side to access the cemetery. Again, the cemetery is about the same size in land as the church itself.

*What's Next?*

San José Mission is located about 15 miles north of San Jose on the highway to Oakland. It will take you about 1 hour to get to the next mission: San Francisco de Asís.

# 19. San Francisco de Asís Mission

3321 16th Street | San Francisco, CA 94114
Phone: (415) 621-8203 | www.missiondolores.org
Museum Hours: 10:00am - 4:00pm
Mondays: Closed

*Fun Facts:*

San Francisco de Asís (Mission Dolores), the 6th Mission, was founded by Father Palóu on June 29, 1776. The mission was named after St. Francis of Assisi, founder of the Franciscan Order, in Assisi, Italy.

The mission is the oldest building in the city. It survived several earthquakes, remaining intact.

Do not confuse Mission Dolores Basilica (the large basilica on the corner) with the actual mission.

*Visiting Time: (about 1 hour)*

You'll have to find parking on the street. Go to the gift shop to purchase your admission. Like I said before, many chapels look similar, but your challenge is to look for the differences. It is easy to spot the beams that are painted in beautifully patterned colors that match the altar. Like San Jose Mission, the original redwood logs that support the roof are fastened together with rawhide. Mission Dolores Chapel is the narrowest: 22 feet wide.

Next door to the mission chapel you can access the Basilica, the parish church. We enjoyed viewing the stained glass with the 21 California missions all around. The pictures I took didn't come out well due to the lighting, but the stained-glass illustrations are a delight to view.

From the Basilica, go to the museum, where you'll see a model of the mission as it was built, the now-missing quadrangle being on the side of the Basilica. You'll then see vestments, mass artifacts, and various paintings.

From the museum, go to the cemetery. In the cemetery, you'll find a display of Indian housing, similar to the one displayed at Mission San Diego:

*What's Next?*

Consider taking an extra day or two to visit the city. There are many places you can visit: The Golden Gate Bridge, Lombard Street, Fisherman's Wharf, a tour of Alcatraz Island, a ride on the Cable Cars, the Painted Ladies, countless museums, Silicon Valley (if you're into technology), so plan accordingly.

San Francisco Mission is located in the city of San Francisco. It will take you about 35 minutes to get to the next mission: San Rafael Arcángel.

# 20. San Rafael Arcángel Mission

1104 5th Street | San Rafael, CA 94901
Phone: (415) 454-8141 | www.saintraphael.com
Museum Hours: 9:00am – 4:00pm

*Fun Facts:*

San Rafael Arcángel, the 20th Mission, was founded by Father Sarría on December 14, 1817. The mission was named after Saint Raphael the Archangel, the angel of bodily healing.

San Rafael was founded as an asistencia (assistance) to serve as a hospital for San Francisco neophytes (Indians newly converted to Catholicism) suffering from depression and disease.

The star window was modeled after Carmel. San Rafael Mission was the first specialized hospital in California.

*Visiting Time: (less than 1 hour)*

You'll have to find parking on the street. As with San Francisco de Asís Mission, do not confuse the mission with the large church facing the street —even if it has the same type of star-window above its doors:

The actual mission chapel is on your right-hand side as you face the above-pictured church. Look for the star window and the bells hanging from a small wooden frame on one side. The gift shop and the museum are behind the mission chapel. Walk up the steep slope and turn right.

The museum has examples of various artifacts and paintings. In one corner, you will see the three original mission bells:

Even though Mission San Rafael was originally designed as a sub-mission, it began to grow and became a full-fledged mission, with a growing population of Indians, as well as cattle and land for agriculture. One detail to note is that there was never a quadrangle at this mission. The main goal was to take advantage of the warmer climate in the area to help those who became ill due to the harsh and foggy weather in San Francisco.

Exit the museum and go back down into the chapel. At the main altar is a statue of Saint Raphael. We were told that the original chapel's floor was dirt, there were no windows and there were no pews.

San Rafael Mission was the first mission to be secularized in 1834. It fell into despair soon after that. Today, San Rafael Mission is one of the smallest, probably the quickest one to visit: less than 1 hour. It is known as the "most obliterated of California's missions."

In 1940, the Hearst Foundation provided the funds to build a replica of the original 1818 building.

*What's Next?*

San Rafael Mission is located 30 minutes north of San Francisco, in the city of San Rafael. It will take you about 35 minutes to get to the next mission: San Francisco Solano.

# 21. San Francisco Solano Mission

114 East Spain St | Sonoma, CA 95476
Phone: (707) 938-9560
www.missionscalifornia.com/keyfacts/san-francisco-
solano.html
Museum Hours: 10:00am - 5:00pm

*Fun Facts:*

San Francisco Solano (in Sonoma), the 21st Mission, was founded by Father Altimira on July 4, 1823. The mission was named after a Spanish saint who was a missionary in the Peruvian Missions.

Solano was the only mission founded after Mexico gained independence from Spain, and the only one founded without approval from the church. It existed for 11 years.

The Sonoma Barracks are located across the street, west of the mission. Solano Mission is part of the Sonoma State Historical Park.

The first California bear flag was raised there on July 14, 1846, proclaiming California a republic and declaring independence from Mexico.

*Visiting Time: (about 1 hour)*

After paying your entry fee, proceed to the museum, where you will see a window into the wall: it shows you the original building blocks of the mission. You can also see some original roof tiles as well as other artifacts.

Continue to the next room where you'll see paintings of 17 of the 21 mission of the Jorgensen Memorial Collection:

As it is the case with La Purisima Mission, Solano Mission is part of a State Park. As such, they are the only two chapels that currently have no pews.

Looking for differences, notice that the columns at the altar are not real; they are actually painted on the wall.

Exit the chapel and go out to the courtyard. Here you can appreciate plants that may have been grown in the mission era. The fountain is in the center, (behind us in the next picture). A little to the right, we were told that where the cactus is, the women's quarters (monjerio) and workstations were located.

*What's Next?*

If you'd like to visit the rest of the Sonoma Historical Park, it should take you about 2 additional hours. You should also plan on walking around the neighborhood, eat at a local restaurant, or go shopping.

Solano Mission is located 30 minutes north of San Francisco, in the city of Sonoma. It will take you about 35 minutes to get to the "Welcome to Napa Valley" south sign, about 25 miles away. Continue driving north to Napa County and consider visiting a winery.

This concludes our visit to all 21 California Missions. We can now say: ***Missions Accomplished!***

And now...

# Can You Name the Missions?

The following 21 pages are for you to write about the California Missions. I have drawn and painted all 21 California Missions on the computer and I have included them here, in order, from San Diego to Sonoma.

In each page, write the following:
- Top of the Page: Write the name of the mission.
- Write one or more facts about that mission, your favorite characteristic(s), or just write down notes.
- Does the mission resemble any other? Which one? How?
- How is it different from others?
- When you visit this mission, describe your visit!
- Get the mission page stamped, place a sticker on it, or glue a paper souvenir.
Enjoy!

1. _____

_____
_____
_____
_____
_____
_____
_____
_____
_____
_____
_____
_____

2. _____

*PaulRallion.com*

_____
_____
_____
_____
_____
_____
_____
_____
_____
_____
_____
_____

3. _____

_____
_____
_____
_____
_____
_____
_____
_____
_____
_____
_____

4. _____

_____
_____
_____
_____
_____
_____
_____
_____
_____
_____
_____

5. _____

_____
_____
_____
_____
_____
_____
_____
_____
_____
_____
_____

6. _____

_____
_____
_____
_____
_____
_____
_____
_____
_____
_____
_____

7. _____

_____
_____
_____
_____
_____
_____
_____
_____
_____
_____
_____

8. _____

_____
_____
_____
_____
_____
_____
_____
_____
_____
_____
_____
_____

9. _____

_____
_____
_____
_____
_____
_____
_____
_____
_____
_____
_____

10. _____

_____
_____
_____
_____
_____
_____
_____
_____
_____
_____
_____

11. _____

_____
_____
_____
_____
_____
_____
_____
_____
_____
_____

12. _____

_____
_____
_____
_____
_____
_____
_____
_____
_____
_____
_____
_____

13. _____

_____
_____
_____
_____
_____
_____
_____
_____
_____
_____
_____
_____

14. _____

_____
_____
_____
_____
_____
_____
_____
_____
_____
_____
_____
_____

15. _____

_____
_____
_____
_____
_____
_____
_____
_____
_____
_____
_____

16. _____

_____
_____
_____
_____
_____
_____
_____
_____
_____
_____
_____

17. _____

_____
_____
_____
_____
_____
_____
_____
_____
_____
_____
_____

18. _____

_____
_____
_____
_____
_____
_____
_____
_____
_____
_____
_____

19. _____

_____
_____
_____
_____
_____
_____
_____
_____
_____
_____
_____

20. _____

_____
_____
_____
_____
_____
_____
_____
_____
_____

21. _____

_____
_____
_____
_____
_____
_____
_____
_____
_____
_____
_____

# Quick Facts

1. San Diego de Alcalá, the first mission and State cemetery.
2. San Luis Rey de Francia, the largest and most populous.
3. San Juan Capistrano, the first vineyard and wine in the State.
4. San Gabriel Arcángel, over 25,000 baptisms were done.
5. San Fernando Rey, its convent is the largest freestanding adobe building in California.
6. San Buenaventura, the only mission to use wooden bells.
7. Santa Bárbara, the only mission that has two bell towers.
8. Santa Inés (in Solvang), home of California's first Seminary.
9. La Purísima Concepción (in Lompoc), built into a linear series of buildings with 37 rooms.
10. San Luis Obispo, the first one to use red roof tiles.
11. San Miguel Arcángel, has no bell tower.
12. San Antonio de Padua, the first marriage in California.
13. Nuestra Señora de Soledad, its original quadrangle is gone.
14. San Carlos Borromeo (in Carmel), Father Serra and Father Lasuén are buried there.
15. San Juan Bautista, sits on the San Andreas Fault.
16. Santa Cruz, half-sized replica built.
17. Santa Clara de Asís, site of the 1st University in California.
18. San José (in Fremont), used as a general store during the Gold Rush.
19. San Francisco de Asís, the oldest building in San Francisco.
20. San Rafael Arcángel, was originally built as a hospital.
21. San Francisco de Solano (in Sonoma), the last mission.
22. Santa Rosa was going to be the 22nd mission.

# Conclusion

Having visited all 21 California Missions is a special trip that not many people have experienced. It takes quite a bit of time to plan, but the experience is well worth it. It is my hope to help you make your planning easier.

Here are some tips you might use:
-    Bring along a tripod and set a timer on a self-shooting camera so that all members of the party appear on the souvenir pictures.
-    Admission Fees: In order to take a tour at the Mission museums, you'll need to pay a fee between $3 and $10 per adult. Most Missions accept credit cards.
-    Consider buying a souvenir at every Mission. You never know when you'll return to them.

The architecture of the missions has influenced commercial buildings as well as residences. Think of the arched corridors and red tile roofs you see in many communities.

As you go through these historical jewels, you wonder about the things that happened in the past. The 65-year Mission period came and went. Our time will also become history, like theirs. I wonder what people will say about our time, say 250 years from now. What do you think things will be like then?

# References

1. Charm Kraft Industries, Inc. (2010). Missions of California. Featuring all 21 Old Spanish Missions.

2. California Missions, A Historic Journey Up El Camino Real to All 21 California Missions [Documentary Series] Howser, Huell (2000).

3. California Missions Resource Center website: www.missionscalifornia.com

4. California Missions Foundation Website: www.californiamissionsfoundation.org

5. Simondi, Thomas E. General Browsing: "MissionTour.org" *Mission Tour Website.* 2001-2015. www.missiontour.org (August 1, 2016)

6. Every Mission's website, whose URL (Universal Resource Locator) appears at the beginning of each Mission's section in this book.

7. Spanish Missions in California. In Wikipedia: https://en.wikipedia.org/wiki/Spanish_missions_in_California

8. Google Maps – www.maps.google.com

# Discussion Notes

The advantage of studying the missions prior to visiting them is that you know what to look for as you go through them. You can look for things described in this book, or even things I did not include.

The path that takes you through the following missions: San Luis Obispo, San Miguel, San Antonio de Padua, Mission Soledad, and Carmel Mission, skips a few attractions, which are out of the way. Consider making alternate plans to visit these locations: Morro Bay, Cayucos State Beach, Hearst Castle, Elephant Seal Viewing Point, and Big Sur.

San Miguel Mission is the "closest" mission to Sequoia and Kings Canyon National Park, which is located about 150 miles, or 2.5 hours northeast. You would need about two to three days to visit those parks.

San José Mission is the closest mission to Yosemite National Park, which is located 140 miles east, or about 3 hours. You would need at least two full days to visit that park.

If you're interested in visiting those parks, check out my other book titled: Sequoia, Kings Canyon, Yosemite National Parks, Visiting Central California, at www.paulrallion.com

Missions Project Recommendations:
If you're a parent of a 4th grader, I can recommend a few missions for your mission project:

San Diego: If you want to show the chain of missions started.

San Luis Rey: If you want to study the largest mission.

Solano: If you want to do the last mission founded.

My daughter has two suggestions as well:

La Purisima: If you like an open-nature environment.

San Carlos Borromeo: If you want to show Father Serra's and Father Lasuén's graves.

I'll leave you with text from a Plaque at Solano Mission:
"The End of the Mission Trail (1523-1823)
The Mission Trail marked 300 years of Spanish-Mexican settlement. It travelled as far south as Guatemala and traversed Mexico to advance through 11 of our present-day United States. In 1823, Mission San Francisco Solano was founded, marking the last and northernmost outpost on the Historic Mission Trail."

# Author's Note

Writing this book has been a reflective experience that took me back to the wonderful journey of visiting all 21 California Missions. During that time, I developed a deeper interest in the missions, and what's unique about each. I have enjoyed reliving those visits and publishing to share with my family, friends, and anyone who is interested in the missions.

By no means do I consider myself an expert in the history of the missions. However, I take pride in my dedication to learn more about them. I have confidence that my book will help you become familiar with them before you visit the missions, or confirm what you see after you visit them.

Finally, I would like to thank my family for supporting me in this project. I would also like to thank you, the reader. I hope that you have enjoyed reading about my experience in visiting all 21 missions.

Do not hesitate to contact me with your feedback or to share your own experiences with me. My e-mail address is paulrallion@gmail.com. For more information, please visit my website: www.paulrallion.com

**Quick Note:** If you found this book helpful, will you please leave a review? Use this QR (quick response) code:

Thank you!

# About the Author

Paul speaks Spanish, English, French, Portuguese, and some Italian. He earned a master's degree in education, is a computer technology National Board Certified teacher, and a Google Educator.

Preview and purchase his books at: PaulRallion.com

1. California Missions, Visiting All 21 (available in Spanish, French, Portuguese, and Italian),
2. London, Paris, Rome, Visiting All 3 (available in Spanish),
3. Sequoia, Kings Canyon, and Yosemite National Parks (available in Spanish),
4. Romance Languages: Spanish, French, Portuguese, Italian,
5. Money & Credit 101 (available in Spanish),
6. My COMPUTeachER, The Computer Book for Everyone,
7. Middle School 101, 101 Tips for Teachers,
8. Middle School 201, More Tips for Teachers,
9. Middle School Parents, Supporting Your Child (available in Spanish),
10. Tips for Life, 101 Ways to Live Better (available in Spanish),
11. Kick Smokin', One Butt at a Time (available in Spanish, French, Portuguese, and Italian),
12. Middle Schoolin', 50 Stories about the Challenges, Humor and Rewards of Teaching,
13. Turning Point, Free Education for the Willing,
14. Middle Schoolers, 50 Tips for Students

Made in the USA
Coppell, TX
14 April 2024

31290586R00075